DREAMING

And I took the night train to the country where nothing lasts,
and it stopped at the night market where nothing is sold,
where all is given and nothing is given for keeps,
And I got some cheese. And it shone like a blue moon,
And a dream-mouse ate my cheese, so I kept the mouse,
and a dream-cat ate my mouse, so I kept the cat,
and a dream-dog chased my cat, so I kept the dog,
and a dream-wolf chased my dog, so I kept the wolf,
and a dream-hunter shot my wolf, so I followed the hunter,
and a dream-horse stole his heart, so I jumped on behind,
and it carried us both toward the watchtowers of morning,
and I took the morning train to my own country,
and it stopped in my own room where nothing changes,
where the mouse sleeps in its hole and the cat sleeps on my bed,
where the dog at the door twitches, dreaming of wolves,
where wolf, hunter, and horse fold up with the shadows,
and I brought back nothing except this story.

NANCY WILLARD

IN BED

When I am in bed
I hear
footsteps of the night
sharp
like the crackling of a dead leaf
in the stillness

Then my mother laughs
downstairs

CHARLOTTE ZOLOTOW

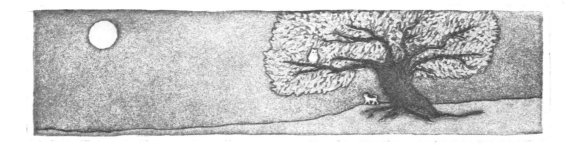

My sister says
I shouldn't color
Rhinos purple,
Hippos green.
She says
I shouldn't be so stupid;
Those are things
She's never seen.
But I don't care
What my sister says,
I don't care
What my sister's seen.
I will color
What I want to—
Rhinos purple,
Hippos green.

MICHAEL PATRICK HEARN

HOMEWORK

What is it about homework
That makes me want to write
My Great Aunt Myrt to thank her for
The sweater that's too tight?

What is it about homework
That makes me pick up socks
That stink from days and days of wear,
Then clean the litter box?

What is it about homework
That makes me volunteer
To take the garbage out before
The bugs and flies appear?

What is it about homework
That makes me wash my hair
And take an hour combing out
The snags and tangles there?

What is it about homework?
You know, I wish I knew,
'Cause nights when I've got homework
I've got much too much to do!

JANE YOLEN

"I'm sorry, Mom."—Sail through my broth...
"Be careful, child, you'll splash your jeans!
 There now, see what you've done! You've spilled
 Food on my nice clean tablecloth!"
"I'm sorry, Mom,"—I think I'll build
 A Pharaoh's Pyramid with beans.

 First make a square, and then along
 The edges lay them stone by stone...
"Don't use your fingers, darling—stop!"
 Why is it always me that's wrong?
 I'm sure I've often seen my Pop
 Pick up and gnaw a meaty bone.

 Yet if I tell her that, she'll say,
"Don't talk, child, with your mouth full!"—Worst,
 They do make eating such a bore,
 When it's so much more fun to play.
 There now, I've dropped some on the floor—
 I hope the puppy finds it first.

                              J. A. LINDON

TROUBLE WITH DINNER

Why can't I dig with my spoon and make
Potato castles like on the beach?
Why aren't there sensible things to eat,
Like jam and jelly and pink-iced cake?
Why stuff like horrid cabbage and meat?
Why can't I kneel on my chair and reach?

It's quicker than saying, "Pass the sauce,"
When nobody listens and nobody will:
And such bad manners to wave or SHOUT,
And wrong to get down and fetch it, of course!
Why shouldn't I "mess my dinner about"
With Gravy River round Spinach Hill?

My knife's a dagger, my fork's a torch,
These peas are PILLS with a POISON label!
I'm Special Agent, the Prince's twin!
My mouth's a secret door in a porch,
Nobody can see what's going in—
"Just take those elbows off the table!"

She bites my arm. She starts to cry.
Then mom would come and the fur would fly!
"No more TV till you kids behave!"
Would be the order mother gave.

"Now to your rooms! Get a book to read—
Get up! Get out! At once! Proceed!"
We'd go to our rooms, but pretty soon,
Sis would sneak back to her darn cartoon.

But I wouldn't care, 'cause I'd started in
To read a book about Huck Finn.
And I thought, "Oh, let her have her way."
I'd read about Huck Finn the rest of the day.

And the next, and the next, and the next, and then
I'd read the book all over again.
And then Tom Sawyer, which I like as well—
I'd read and read till the dinner bell.

Then I got more books and pretty soon,
I'd read away all afternoon.
Books are the things that are best for me—
My sister can have her old TV!

WILLIAM COLE

Did you ever fight with your sister? Yes?
I did, a year ago—or less;
We'd never come to the same decision
'Bout what to watch on television.

She was a Woody Woodpecker fan,
And me—I wanted Superman;
I was stronger—that didn't help,
'Cause she was louder—how she'd yelp!

So every day the house would rock
When it came around to four o'clock—
I think a kid is full of prunes
Who wants to watch those dumb cartoons.

"I don't want Superman! I want Woody!"
"Oh, shut up, you goody-goody!"
"Hey, ma, look! He took my seat!"
"Why don't you kids watch Sesame Street?"

"But that's no good—we're both too old!"
"You're making my hair turn gray!" Ma'd scold.
I change the channel. Sis pulls the plug.
I pin her down upon the rug.

NEIGHBORS

The Cobbles live in the house next door,
In the house with the prickly pine.
Whenever I see them, they ask, "How are you?"
And I always answer, "I'm fine."
And I always ask them, "Is Jonathan home?"
(Jonathan Cobble is nine.)
I'm Jonathan Cobble's very best friend
And Jonathan Cobble is mine.

MARY ANN HOBERMAN

JUMPING ROPE

This started out as a
   jumping rope
You prob'ly think that
   I'm a dope
But this started out as a
   jumping rope
And now I fear there is
   no hope
But this started out as a
   jumping rope.

SHEL SILVERSTEIN

SNACK

Give me a sandwich—
   cheese or ham;
Guess you don't know
   how hungry I am.

Give me a hamburger,
   dill pickle too;
Mustard on top—
   that will do.

Plate of French fries,
   catsup red;
Yes, I'm hungry—
   that's what I said!

LOIS LENSKI

CLASSROOM

Boredom

I stare at
The number 2

I stare at
The number 2

I stare at
The number 2

It looks
Like a swan!

KENNETH GANGEMI

IN THE LIBRARY

You're right:
I am too old for THIS,
But I like pictures in my book,
And lots of color, easy words—
You needn't give me such a look!
You're wrong:
I am too young for THAT;
The words are long, the type's too small,
I don't find any pictures there—
I'd never get through that at all!

MICHAEL PATRICK HEARN

Jenny The Juvenile Juggler

Jenny had hoops she could sling in the air
And she brought them along to the Summerhill Fair.
And a man from a carnival sideshow was there,
Who declared that he needed a juggler.

And it's
   Oops! Jenny, whoops! Jenny,
   Swing along your hoops, Jenny,
   Spin a little pattern as you go;
Because it's
   Oops! Jenny's hoops! Jenny,
   Sling a loop-the-loop, Jenny,
   Whoops! Jenny, oops! Jenny, O!

Well, the man was astonished at how the hoops flew,
And he said, "It's amazing what some kids can do!"
And now at the carnival, Act Number Two
Is Jenny the Juvenile Juggler.

And it's
   Oops! Jenny, whoops! Jenny,
   Swing along your hoops, Jenny,
   Spin a little pattern as you go;
Because it's
   Oops! Jenny's hoops! Jenny,
   Sling a loop-the-loop, Jenny,
   Whoops! Jenny, oops! Jenny, O!

DENNIS LEE

Freddy

Here is the story
Of Freddy, my friend,
Who ran out in the traffic,
And that is the end.

Double-Barrelled Ding-Dong-Bat

Why,
You—

Double-barrelled,
Disconnected,
Supersonic
Ding-dong-bat:

Don't you dare come
Near me, or I'll
Disconnect you
Just like that!

LUNCH

For Plate Lunch today, I have six different choices,
Six different choices for lunches today:

The menu says Hamburger Steak with brown gravy,
   peas on the side and a pineapple slice.
The menu says Chili con Carne with crackers—
   I've already had it for lunch this week—twice!
The menu says Meatloaf—it, too, has brown gravy,
   beets on the side and a salad of slaw.
The menu says Fish Sticks with tarter sauce topping,
   and shoestring potatoes—they taste just like straw.
The menu says Tacos—right here, it says Tacos,
   but you'd never know from their shape or their size.
And finally the menu, way down at the bottom,
   says Green Noodles smothered with Chicken Surprise!

How can I choose with such choices to choose from?
Which of these lunches should I have today?

KATY HALL

BRINNNNNNNNG.
The cold sharp bell
chases me into the hall
and all the sea things
into hidden corners.
I leave the sea behind,
waiting till next week,
but in the distance
I know
one small fish
follows me home.

JOANNE RYDER

My math's in my pocket,
my pencil is here
in my hair where I put it
in back of my ear.
I tripped and I dropped it.
It dropped and I kicked it.
I kicked it and stopped it.
It's near
where?
There
here.

I get to the corner.
I stop at the corner.
The light at the corner
goes green with a wink.
The bell begins ringing
and I begin running.
I run
and it's ringing.
I made it . . .
I think.

KARLA KUSKIN

Inside the lab
all the living things are quiet.
Some read, some scratch,
some rest inside a leaf.
Only the sea is beating
steadily, softly
inside the fragile tank,
inside me.

While everybody studies,
I watch white octopi
skitter from the pages
to the smooth dark floor
where small silver fish
nibble sweetly
at a piece of fallen chalk.
No one notices the eels
swim singlefile
down the rows to deeper waters,
or sees that right behind
our teacher's head
shy seahorses bob
up and down and up,
peeking at me.
I tuck my legs under my chair
and let the sharks slide by,
I can almost touch them.

GOING TO SCHOOL

From here to there
or anywhere
is longer in the morning.
It doesn't seem so far by blocks
but first I have to find some socks
that match.
I have to brush this
and tie those
and tuck that.
There's a clock on the wall
ticking, "Hurry don't fall,"
as I run down the hall.
Well, I won't fall at all.

Out the door
down the block.
"Good morning tree,
hello there rock,"
(In my head the ticking clock).
I'm running
I'm walking
I watch a cat stalking a bird
through the bushes
but I'm on my way.
I know I'm not yet there
I never may get there
with small stones for kicking
and weeds for picking.
That dog down the block
lobs a bark at the day.

EGG THOUGHTS

Soft-Boiled

I do not like the way you slide,
I do not like your soft inside,
I do not like you many ways,
And I could do for many days
Without a soft-boiled egg.

Sunny-Side-Up

With their yolks and whites all runny
They are looking at me funny.

Sunny-Side-Down

Lying face-down on the plate
On their stomachs there they wait.

Poached

Poached eggs on toast, why do you shiver
With such a funny little quiver?

Scrambled

I eat as well as I am able,
But some falls underneath the table.

Hard-Boiled

With so much suffering today
Why do them any other way?

RUSSELL HOBAN

CRAZY QUILT

The early sunlight quilts the floor,
FLOWER GARDEN, BROKEN STAR,
From the window to the door,
DOUBLE WEDDING RING.

The patterns echo in my head,
SEVEN SISTERS, DRUNKARD'S PATH,
They comfort me when I'm in bed,
DOUBLE WEDDING RING.

And when it's time to start the day,
Get up, go out, to school or play,
I know that on my bed will be
My Crazy Quilt awaiting me:
FLOWER GARDEN,
BROKEN STAR,
SEVEN SISTERS,
DRUNKARD'S PATH,
OLD LOG CABIN,
And THE WRENCH,
DOUBLE WEDDING RING.

JANE YOLEN

AT DAWN

I know I dreamed again last night.
I don't recall exactly what
Awoke me in the dead of night.
The only thing I'm certain's that
I'm grateful for the morning light.

MICHAEL PATRICK HEARN

For Louise Porter Fear,
"Nanny"
M.P.H.

For Marilyn
B.G.

Acknowledgments

We thank the following for permission to reprint the material listed below:

William Cole for "Let Her Have it!" Copyright © 1981 by William Cole.

Thomas Y. Crowell for "In Bed" from RIVER WINDING by Charlotte Zolotow.
Text copyright © 1970 by Charlotte Zolotow.

Curtis Brown, Ltd., for "Crazy Quilt" by Jane Yolen. Copyright © 1981 by Jane Yolen; "Homework" by Jane Yolen.
Copyright © 1981 by Jane Yolen.

Kenneth Gangemi for "Classroom" from LYDIA by Kenneth Gangemi. Text copyright © 1970 by Kenneth Gangemi.

Katy Hall for "Lunch." Copyright © 1981 by Katy Hall.

Harper & Row, Publishers, Inc., for "Egg Thoughts" from EGG THOUGHTS AND OTHER FRANCIS SONGS by Russell Hoban.
Text copyright © 1964, 1972 by Russell Hoban.

Harper & Row, Publishers, Inc., for "Jumping Rope" from WHERE THE SIDEWALK ENDS by Shel Silverstein.
Copyright © 1974 by Shel Silverstein

Michael Patrick Hearn and McIntosh & Otis, Inc., for "At Dawn." Copyright © 1981 by Michael Patrick Hearn;
"In the Library." Copyright © 1981 by Michael Patrick Hearn; "Rhinos Purple, Hippos Green."
Copyright © 1981 by Michael Patrick Hearn.

Karla Kuskin for "Going to School." Copyright © 1981 by Karla Kuskin.

Dennis Lee for SCHOOLYARD RIMES: "Double-Barrelled Ding-Dong-Bat." Copyright © 1981 by Dennis Lee; "Freddy."
Copyright © 1981 by Dennis Lee; "Jenny the Juvenile Juggler." Copyright © 1981 by Dennis Lee.

J.A. Lindon for "Trouble with Dinner." Copyright © 1981 by J. A. Lindon.

Russell & Volkening, Inc., as agents of the author, for "Neighbors" from HELLO AND GOOD-BY
by Mary Ann Hoberman. Copyright © 1959 by Mary Ann Hoberman.

Joanne Ryder for "Inside the Science Lab." Copyright © 1981 by Joanne Ryder.

Henry Z. Walck, Inc., a division of the David McKay Company, Inc., for "Snack" from CITY POEMS by Lois Lenski.
Text copyright © 1971 by Lois Lenski.

Nancy Willard for "Dreaming." Text copyright © 1981 by Nancy Willard.

Text copyright © 1981 by Frederick Warne and Co., Inc.

Illustrations copyright © 1981 by Barbara Garrison

Frederick Warne & Co., Inc.
New York, New York
Library of Congress Cataloging in Publication Data
Main entry under title:
Breakfast, books, and dreams.
Summary: A collection of 18 poems focusing
on daily activities.
1. Children's poetry, American. 2. Children—Poetry.
[1. American poetry—Collections]
I. Hearn, Michael Patrick. II. Garrison, Barbara.
PS595.C45B7   811'.54'0809282   80-13498
ISBN 0-7232-6189-X

Printed in the U.S.A.
Typography by Kathleen Westray

1   2   3   4   5   85   84   83   82   81

A DAY IN VERSE
BREAKFAST, BOOKS, & DREAMS

by

WILLIAM COLE, KENNETH GANGEMI, KATY HALL,
MICHAEL PATRICK HEARN, RUSSELL HOBAN,
MARY ANN HOBERMAN, KARLA KUSKIN, DENNIS LEE,
LOIS LENSKI, J. A. LINDON, JOANNE RYDER,
SHEL SILVERSTEIN, NANCY WILLARD, JANE YOLEN,
and CHARLOTTE ZOLOTOW

Selected by
MICHAEL PATRICK HEARN

With etchings by
BARBARA GARRISON

FREDERICK WARNE
New York London

BREAKFAST, BOOKS, & DREAMS

J
811.54   Breakfast, books, and
B740   dreams.

822030   APR '82   9.95